Transformational Tools for Educators Workbook

Activities to Beat Burnout

Katrina G. Huels

Applied Harmony

Table of Contents

Beginning the Work
Introduction and Assessment

At its core, the work of an educator is rooted in a deep commitment to student growth. Teachers master content and pedagogy, leaders strive to create inclusive cultures conducive to learning, and support staff work tirelessly to ensure learning and content are accessible to all. Technical skills, leadership, and dedication absolutely matter when it comes to student growth and success, but these things alone do not determine your ability to thrive and excel in your work. If you want to elevate your skills, maintain job satisfaction, avoid burnout, and remain connected to your purpose long-term, cultivating emotional intelligence as a core part of your professional skill set makes the difference between surviving and thriving in the field.[1]

Transformational Tools for Special Educators (Corwin, 2026) synthesizes what research consistently demonstrates: the key to avoiding burnout and sustaining long-term impact in your work rests on the ability to recognize and manage your emotions, navigate relationships effectively, and maintain clarity under pressure.[2] This workbook is designed to develop and strengthen those skills.

The Transformational Tools Workbook provides interactive content aligned with 13 tools proven to build emotional intelligence skills when used consistently. It is designed to support educators across roles, including district and local school leaders, teachers, support staff, and related support professionals. If you own *Transformational Tools for Special Educators*, this workbook effectively bridges the gap between *knowing* and *doing*. If you do not own the book, you will find that there is more than enough information on each selected tool for you to engage fully with this content.

Whether you have come to this workbook independently or through group study, you will experience the greatest benefit by approaching the tools with a willingness to try new ways of cultivating balance, purpose, and joy in the important work that you do. And your work as an educator IS important. You touch countless lives every day, and you hold the potential to make a positive difference, not just for students, but also for families, colleagues, and your community. Simply put, you and your work matter, and it is crucial to adopt solutions that focus on taking care of yourself in the same way that you care for others.

How to Use this Workbook

The Transformational Tools Workbook aligns with the structure and approach of *Transformational Tools for Special Educators* (Corwin, 2026). Readers who own the book will greatly benefit from the seamless alignment of content and organizational structure. However, this resource was designed to stand on its own; it does not require that the published book be used alongside it. As the title suggests, this book was created for all education professionals, and it is applicable across roles and settings.

Intentionally designed to be hands-on and interactive, this workbook presents 13 high-impact emotional intelligence tools, each with a short self-assessment, a review of selected application techniques, and targeted practice and reflection activities. Readers can move through the activities sequentially or jump directly to the sections that speak to their immediate needs. Some activities take just five to ten minutes, while others invite deeper exploration when you or your team have more time. Return to the exercises as often as needed; emotional intelligence develops in layers over time, and each engagement reveals new insight.

The Transformational Tools Workbook is notably well-suited for the following purposes:

- Individual Study
- Professional Development
- Professional Learning Communities
- Educational Leadership Study
- Education Seminars
- New Teacher Resource
- University Education Programs
- Transformational Tools Live and Remote Training

However you choose to use this workbook, remember that it takes time for your brain to develop the neural networks that will support new strategies and behaviors.[3] The best results will always come from using your chosen tools consistently, over time.

Let's Assess

Emotional intelligence development is greatly beneficial to anyone, but many readers are drawn to *Transformational Tools for Special Educators* because of its subtitle: *How to Beat Burnout and Become the Best at What You Do*. If preventing or overcoming burnout applies to you, it is important to know that symptoms of burnout and its precursors are not static. They range from low to severe, and certain emotional states can quickly move you to the higher end of the burnout continuum.

Let's take a moment to assess your current levels of stress or burnout. The better you understand your current state, the more precise you can be in your selection of tools. The key to making the most out of this workbook is to choose strategies and activities that best match your personal needs right now.

Several online inventories will provide insight into your current burnout levels:

- The Maslach Burnout Inventory (MBI)
- Oldenburg Burnout Inventory (OBI)
- The Copenhagen Burnout Inventory (CBI)

Bear in mind that all of these options provide a snapshot of how burnout may be affecting you in the present moment. None of the inventories provides diagnoses, and they are intended only to give you clarity about your current experience.

For our purposes, I encourage you to take the Educator Energy and Recovery Check (EERC) included in this introduction (p. x), along with the MBI via www.maslachburnout.com, which you can complete online at no cost. Once you complete both assessments and have your scores, log them in the table provided. Then, mark your calendar to retake your assessments three and six months after your initial inventory so that you can measure your progress.

Date	MBI Scores	EERC Scores	Notes
Baseline			
3 Months			
6 Months			

Let's Get Started

The Transformational Tools Workbook is divided into two parts. In Part One, we will explore activities aligned with the inner domains of emotional intelligence: self-awareness, self-regulation, and internal motivation, because developing internal skills first lays a stronger foundation for the successful execution of external skills.[4] In Part Two, we move into activities that focus on the external emotional intelligence domains: empathy and social skills.

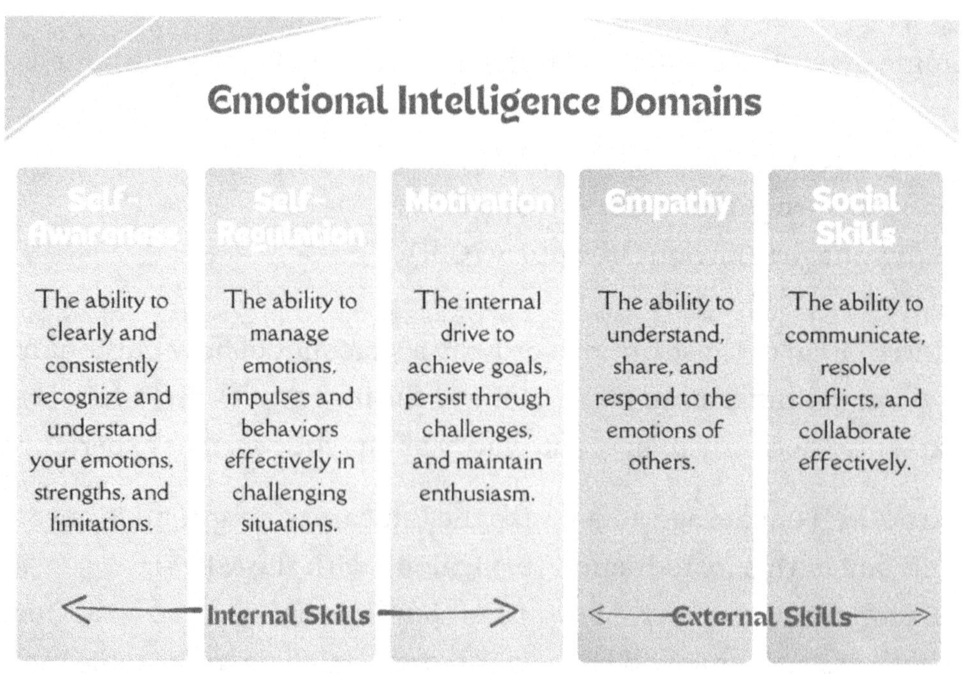

Designated chapters present information on curated tools for each emotional intelligence domain:

- Self-awareness: Chapter Two
- Self-regulation: Chapter Three
- Motivation: Chapter Four
- Empathy: Chapter Six
- Social Skills: Chapter Seven

For each of these chapters, check-in activities prompt you to think about your current level of mastery, followed by selected tools for each domain and specific techniques for application. Interactive practice activities engage active learning so that you understand how to implement the tools effectively and correctly. Finally, each chapter ends with a structured reflection that consolidates learning, reinforces insight, and supports intentional integration into professional practice.

🔍 TIPS

- Most of the tools and techniques provided here can be easily integrated into your daily schedule. For best results, determine a time of day that you will integrate a specific practice, then mark your calendar or set an alarm to trigger engagement.
- Several techniques are provided for each tool, so if one technique is not integrating easily for you, it is perfectly okay to choose another technique that better suits your needs.
- At the end of each day or at the end of the week, take time to reflect on any positive changes you noticed from using the tools. This reinforces your effort and motivates you to continue.
- Should you get off track and forget to integrate the strategies, do not give up! Just pick up where you left off and keep moving.

Educator Energy and Recovery Check

Purpose:
This brief self check helps you notice patterns in work energy, alignment with values, and day to day recovery. It is intended for personal reflection only. It is not a diagnostic tool and it is not a substitute for medical or mental health care.

Instructions:
Read each statement and rate how often this has been true for you over the past two weeks. Use the following scale:

1=Never
2=Rarely
3=Sometimes
4=Often
5=Always

Scoring:
Add your numbers for a total score ranging from 12 to 60. Higher totals indicate stronger alignment and recovery with lower strain.

48 to 60 suggest generally sustainable patterns with targeted tuning.

36 to 47 suggest mixed patterns where one or more areas may need focused support.

12 to 35 suggest frequent strain and limited recovery and call for immediate attention to workload, boundaries, and self regulation routines.

I maintain my energy level throughout my workday. ☐

My level of patience with students and colleagues is consistent. ☐

My daily tasks reflect why I chose this profession. ☐

The way success is measured at my school fits my core values. ☐

Outside of work I am able to be present with people who matter to me. ☐

I do not notice physical symptoms like tight shoulders or headaches during my workday. ☐

I can name at least one moment each day that feels meaningful in my role. ☐

I usually end the day feeling ready to return to work tomorrow. ☐

When a day goes poorly I can recover by the next morning. ☐

My workload feels manageable. ☐

My work culture feels collaborative and inclusive. ☐

I get enough rest and sleep well. ☐

Reflection Activity

- How do your MBI results compare with your EERC scores? Where do the assessments align, and where do they differ?

- Based on your scores, what is one area that you need to focus on?

- Looking at scores from both assessments, what results surprised you and/or confirmed what you already suspected?

Part One

Internal Mastery

Building the Foundation

Chapter 1
Introduction to Internal Skills

Internal emotional intelligence skills encompass three foundational domains: self-awareness, self-regulation, and motivation. These domains are interconnected, each complementing and reinforcing the others. Self-awareness illuminates what you're feeling and why, bringing unconscious triggers and patterns into conscious view. Self-regulation takes that awareness and channels it into an intentional response, giving you the power to choose how you engage with others, especially in challenging circumstances. Motivation, or your inner drive, sustains you by building resilience and keeping you aligned with what matters most to you.

Building internal mastery lays a strong foundation for outward-facing skills like empathy and social competence. It can be difficult to practice empathy, communicate effectively, or showcase your conflict resolution abilities when your emotions remain unregulated. *Transformational Tools for Special Educators* (Corwin, 2026) uses the analogy of a tree to illustrate this relationship, with internal skills serving as the roots that allow external skills to develop and flourish.

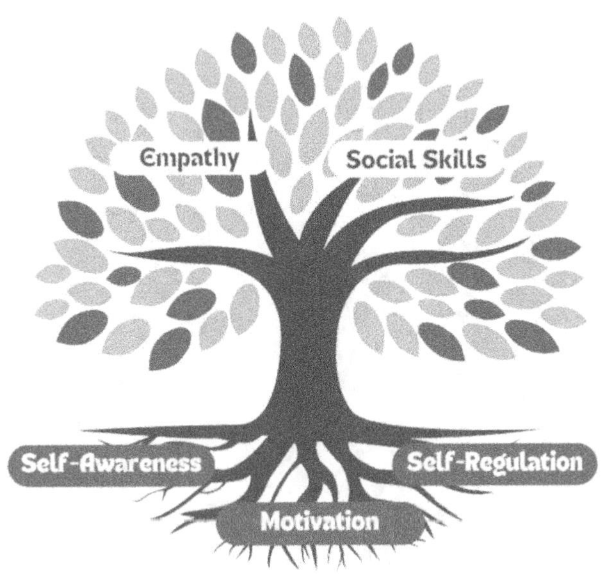

The following chapter begins with self-awareness, where you will use selected tools to recognize and shift the physical sensations of rising emotions before they overwhelm you. Next, self-regulation practices will show you how to interrupt your brain's automatic stress responses, creating space for thoughtful action. Finally, you will reconnect with your professional "why" and learn new ways to set goals and master challenges in both personal and professional settings.

The activities in chapters two, three, and four begin building neural pathways that make internal mastery more automatic over time, rewiring your brain for greater composure, clarity, and resilience. As you work through them, remember that you are not just managing your emotions. **You are transforming them.**

Chapter 2
Self-Awareness Activities

Self-awareness skills transform potentially reactive moments into opportunities for clarity and intentional growth. When you recognize your emotions and identify what triggers them, you create the mental space to choose your response. You begin to anticipate words, circumstances, or behaviors that usually provoke strong reactions for you, and instead of being caught off guard by these emotions, you maintain clarity under pressure and respond with intention.

We will focus on three research-supported self-awareness tools:

✓ **Gratitude Practices**: Shift attention from reactive states to constructive emotions.

✓ **Expressive Writing**: Processes and releases deeper emotions, resulting in a sense of release and balance.

✓ **Affect Labeling**: Precisely naming emotions to bring a shift from reactivity to conscious consideration.

Gratitude Practices

The benefits of shifting your mind towards a state of gratitude cannot be overstated. Research consistently shows that when you experience feelings of thankfulness, stress decreases, mood improves, reward regions in the brain are stimulated, and connections with others are strengthened.[1] Research also shows that daily gratitude practices can improve sleep quality and increase resilience to stress in a relatively short time.[2]

A mental state of gratitude is always available to you, but despite its many benefits, gratitude exercises can be challenging, especially if you are dealing with chronic stress, overwhelm, or fatigue. When any of these conditions are present, finding something positive in your life may seem impossible.

The gratitude activities selected here are effective and easy to use, and they can activate positive feelings even when you struggle to access them. The more you engage, the easier it is to bring gratitude forward, even during emotionally-charged circumstances.

Before learning specific techniques to practice gratitude, take a moment to consider your own experience with this mindset by completing the short questionnaire below.

Gratitude Check

Circle the Best Answer.

1) How often do you experience gratitude?
   Daily   Weekly   Monthly   Never

2) Can you think of one thing that you are thankful for right now?
   Yes   No

3) Have you ever intentionally shifted your mindset to a state of gratitude to reduce stress or anxiety?
   Yes   No

If your answers indicate that you rarely experience gratitude, struggle to find something to be thankful for, or if you have never intentionally shifted into a state of gratitude, consistently integrating these practices will make significant changes in your personal or professional life.

As you move through each gratitude method in the following pages, think about how you might incorporate them into your daily or weekly schedule, then take a moment to answer the questions on page 10.

The Gratitude Jar

- Place an empty jar in a convenient location. Your jar can sit in your workplace, your home, or both.

- Next to the jar, place small strips of paper or card and a pen.

- Each day, write just **one thing** that you are thankful for. It can be something that happened during an activity, or something broader like "friends."

- Set time aside to review randomly selected gratitude notes. Reviews can be weekly, monthly, or whatever frequency best serves your needs. If you do not feel inspired after reading one or two notes, keep going until your mind begins to shift.

Tips

 Your gratitude jar can assist you when finding something to be thankful for is challenging. If you are experiencing stress, fatigue, or if you feel notably pessimistic, just select and read one or more of your notes to stimulate a shift towards a gratitude mindset.

 Choose a jar that is appealing to you. This gives you a positive psychological cue and slightly lowers the effort to add a note.

Gratitude Activation

This powerful technique works by pairing music with intense feelings of gratitude. Practice the following technique once a day - it should take less than ten minutes. After a week or so, you only need to play a specific song to activate intense feelings of gratitude!

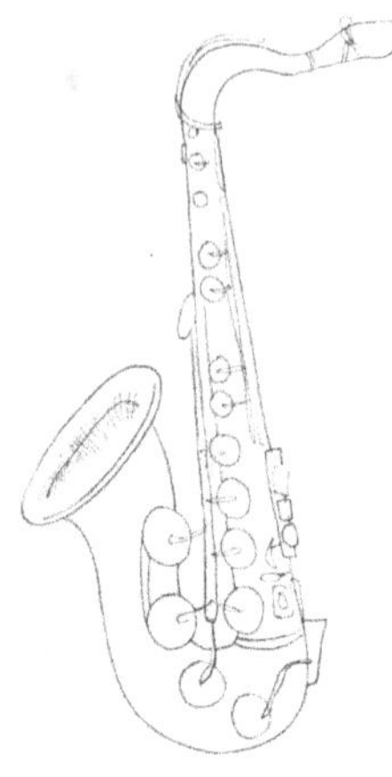

The Process

- Select a song that genuinely uplifts you. Any genre works as long as it sparks joy or inspiration when you hear it. Keep it easily accessible on your phone or device.

- Before pressing play, bring to mind something you're deeply grateful for. This could be a special person, a meaningful moment, a personal achievement, or a period in your life that filled you with joy.

- Start your chosen song and let yourself fully experience the gratitude. Visualize your focal point vividly while the music plays. Don't just think about it; actually feel the warmth and appreciation in your body.

- Allow the music and your grateful feelings to intertwine, creating a powerful emotional anchor between the song and your sense of appreciation.

Activation

If you practice Gratitude Activation daily for at least one week, just hearing the opening notes of your song will automatically trigger feelings of gratitude, giving you instant access to this mindset whenever you need it.

Gratitude Writing 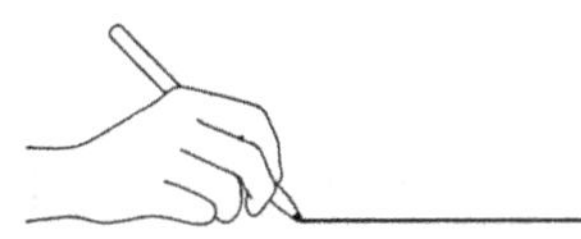

Gratitude writing can be practiced in a variety of ways. From journaling to short thank-you notes, the act of writing down what you are thankful for creates deep engagement with feelings of appreciation, gratitude, and optimism.

Three Good Things

Select a notepad or journal specifically for this practice. At the end of each day, write down three specific things that you are thankful for, and include a date for each entry. If you have a particularly stressful day and find it difficult to recall anything that went well, take a moment to review previous entries. Revisiting former gratitude moments will will gently push you to a more open mindset, making it easier to find your three good things for the day.

Gratitude Letter

Writing a gratitude letter is an excellent practice when feelings of negativity are consistent over time. This practice takes longer than most, but the impact includes a deep shift towards positivity and optimism. Choose one person you are notably grateful for, and write a letter outlining the positive impact the person has had on your life. Be as specific as possible. You can choose to save or share the letter; it is the practice itself that shifts your mindset.

Gratitude Sharing

Choose one to two days a week to write thank-you notes to your colleagues, family members, or friends. To make the practice habitual, choose a certain number of cards to write on a selected weekday. You can schedule this time on your calendar or use an alarm to prompt engagement. When you write your notes, use specific examples like, "I appreciated your support during our weekly meeting" or "Your positive attitude brightens my day." This practice not only boosts your mood and reduces stress, it also strengthens your relationship with others.

Consider the three gratitude practices: The Gratitude Jar, Gratitude Activation, and Gratitude Writing, and use the space below to answer the following questions:

1. Which gratitude practice did you resonate most with?
2. Can you find small pockets of time to include your favorite gratitude method? If so, what time(s) of day will work best?
3. How do you think including a gratitude practice will benefit you?

____

____

____

____

____

____

____

To shift into a state of gratitude, spend a few minutes thinking about one or two people who recently inspired you through their actions. Perhaps they performed an act of kindness, advocacy, or went out of their way to help you or someone else. The act can be great or small - what matters is that it stands out for YOU. Briefly write down the details below.

____

____

____

____

____

____

____

Now write a short but specific thank-you note to the person or people noted above. This can be an email, card, text, or any method you choose. Be sure to include:

- Description of the act
- How you felt upon witnessing or receiving the action
- How the action was significant to you

Once you complete your thank-you notes, consider what effect this exercise had on you mentally and physically by choosing one to three words that describe your current state. Then, add your descriptors to the lines above for reference.

Gratitude practices like these do more than express appreciation to others. They shift your mind and body to a state of balance, and from that calm state, you gain a new perspective.

🔍 **TIPS**

- Implementing a specific gratitude method close to the same time every day will give you the best results. Whether you play your gratitude activation song, write a thank-you note, or add to your gratitude jar, engaging regularly within a specific time frame creates a reliable cue so that your follow-through becomes automatic.

- You can use a single method, all three, or add your own gratitude practice. What matters most is consistent engagement.

Expressive Writing Practices

For most people, emotions tend to accumulate throughout the day. In education, this is even more pronounced because the work is multifaceted and demands layer and shift, often without time to recover between tasks. This can result in physical tension, mental fog, and fatigue. Expressive writing offers a direct pathway to release cumulative emotions in less than 15 minutes.

This practice shifts how your brain processes emotions, releasing emotional overwhelm and fostering a sense of clarity. It is a simple practice, but expressive writing can recalibrate your nervous system and strengthen your capacity to handle future stress, creating a sustainable pattern of emotional management.[3]

Take a moment to consider how your emotions accumulate during a typical workday by completing the short questionnaire below.

Emotional Accumulation Check

Circle the Best Answer.

1) Do you start your day relatively calm, but at the end of the day feel overwhelmed, stressed, or fatigued?

   Yes   No   Sometimes

2) Do you leave work carrying thoughts or feelings that accumulated during the day?

   Yes   No   Sometimes

3) Do you have an outlet to release stress like working out or journaling?

   Yes   No

Although this practice is helpful for anyone, if you answered "yes" to either of the first two questions and "no" to question three, expressive writing will be particularly beneficial to YOU.

The aim of this practice is emotional release, which requires you to set thinking aside while you write. Quieting your mind may feel difficult at first, but with steady practice, your mind will settle as soon as you begin the exercise. Try to keep writing without pause so that you do not analyze, judge, or interpret your words. Ignore grammar, punctuation, and content. Allow yourself to just WRITE.

Expressive Writing

Do not worry about grammar, punctuation, or content while you write. If you feel yourself "thinking," stop, move back to what you are feeling, then resume writing.

Prompted Writing

-Set a timer from 3 to five minutes.

-As yourself a specific question to prompt your writing. For example, "Why do I feel disrespected today?" or "Where are these feelings or irritability coming from?"

-Start the timer and start writing **without trying to answer the question**. The key is to ask the question, and then let yourself write.

Stream-of-Conscious

-Set a timer from 5 to 15 minutes.

-Start the timer and allow your mind to move where it wants to go.

-Begin writing and keep going until the alarm sounds.

Freewriting

-Set a timer from 5 to 15 minutes.

-Focus on the primary emotion that you feel right now.

-Name the emotion, start the timer, and write until the alarm sounds.

The best way to understand the benefits of expressive writing is to try it. Choose one of the three techniques on page 14 and set your timer for five to ten minutes. Have your pen and paper or electronic device ready, and start your timer. Be sure to follow the tips to disregard grammar, punctuation, and avoid analyzing what you write. When you finish your session, answer the reflection questions below.

1. Which expressive writing technique did you choose? Why did you select this method?
2. Were you able to write without "thinking?" If not, were you able to adjust and keep going?
3. Do you feel differently after completing this exercise? If so, how would you describe the difference?
4. If you struggled with this exercise or did not notice an emotional release, are you willing to try it a few more times? If so, when will you try again?

____

____

____

____

____

____

____

Depending on how often your emotions accumulate, you may choose to integrate this practice daily, weekly, or two to three times during the workweek. As with all of the tools provided here, the key is to practice consistently, then assess your progress over time.

Affect Labeling Exercises

Affect labeling is the deliberate act of naming what you feel in a given moment. By giving your feeling(s) a simple, accurate word, you activate attention and language systems that soften the emotional effect, creating room to think. The result is steadier judgment and quicker recovery, even in fast-moving classroom or team settings. A brief pause (three minutes or less) to say "anxious," "irritated," or "disappointed" can immediately interrupt reactivity and restore choice, making affect labeling an invaluable tool for busy educators.

This technique works best when you use precision when naming your emotions. In *Transformational Tools for Special Educators* (Corwin, 2026), techniques to cultivate accurate labels for your emotions include visual emotional charts.[4] There are many such charts available online, often called Feelings Wheels or Emotions Charts, and these can be accessed by a quick browser search. We will offer additional ways to label emotions accurately on page 16, but before exploring them, take a moment to try affect labeling right now by completing the exercise below.

How Do You Feel?

Try this exercise!

1) Set a one minute timer and relax.
2) Name the emotion you are experiencing right now by quietly speaking or writing it.
3) Give your feeling a zero to ten rating.
4) Refine the emotion label to something more exact by moving from a broad description to a more specific one. For example, shift from anxious to uneasy or happy to excited. Say or write the descriptor.
5) Rate your feeling again. Did your rating change?

When you begin labeling your emotions in real-time, you create a steady process of maintaining balance throughout your day. It is a simple yet powerful practice because when you name your feelings, you engage cognition and build a bridge between raw emotion and clear thinking. In just a few moments, emotional intensity decreases, and a sense of clarity takes hold.

Affect Labeling

The effects of affect labeling are more pronounced when emotional labels are specific. Mobile applications that include mood trackers are particularly helpful with emotional specificity, as are dictionaries that focus on identifying emotions accurately.

How We Feel

How We Feel is a **free** mobile application that does not require a subscription and does not run ads while you engage. It offers an easy way to practice affect labeling by starting with a broad feeling then refining it, tap by tap, to a precise emotion label. The app also allows you add details when you check in so that you can uncover emotional patterns over time.

How We Feel was conceived in conjunction with Yale University's Center for Emotional intelligence and based on the work of Dr. Marc Brackett. It is a science-based nonprofit organization.

Emotions Dictionaries

Using an emotions dictionary directly supports affect labeling by guiding you from a vague feeling to the exact word that fits. Each time you research an emotional word, you strengthen the habit of naming feelings accurately, which improves self awareness and regulation.

An excellent iOS option is the *Emotions Dictionary* (illustrated below). *The Dictionary of Emotions: Words For Feelings, Moods, and Emotions* by Patrick Michael Ryan is an additional resource, available on Amazon.

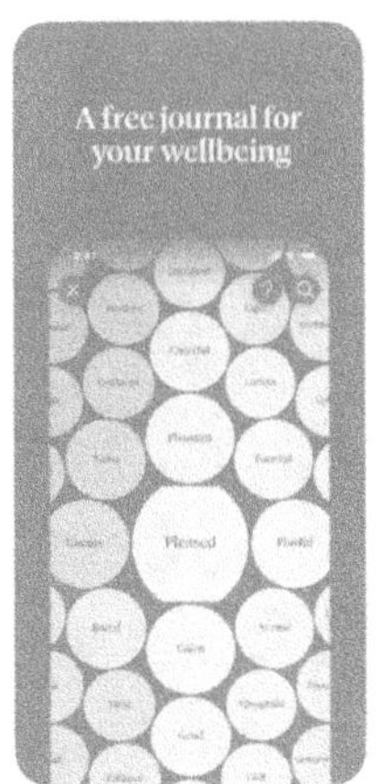

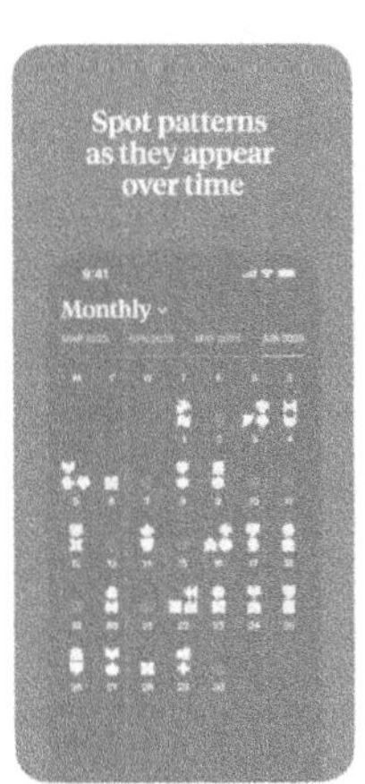

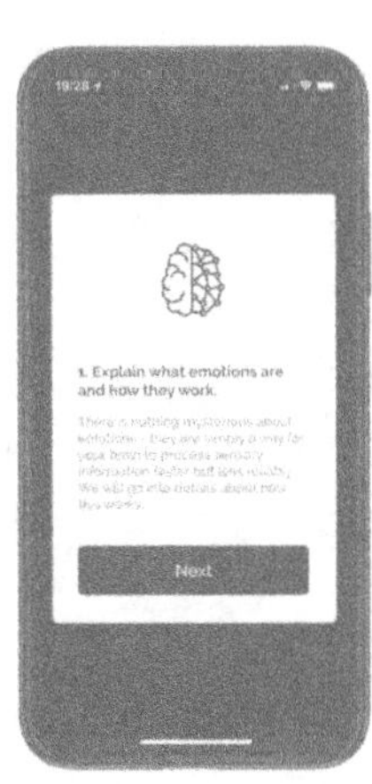

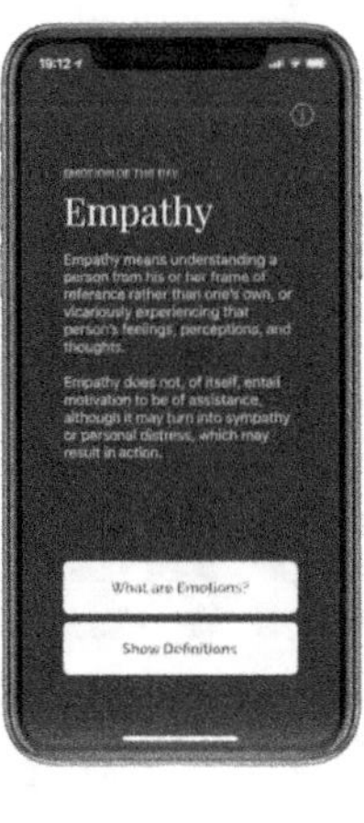

Download the *How We Feel* mobile application and explore the interface, particularly the way you can choose one of the four broad emotion descriptors, then select a specific label to best describe your emotion.

Once you feel comfortable, think about how you are feeling right now and choose one of the broad descriptors: High Energy Unpleasant, High Energy Pleasant, Low Energy Unpleasant, or Low Energy Pleasant, then refine it to the label that best describes your current mood or feeling. If you cannot define your mood with just one of the broad categories or one label, you can choose as many as you need by selecting the "Add Emotion" button next to the date/time button.

Finish by adding what you are doing, who you are with, and where you are, then add physical sensations before you click "Complete check-in."

Once your check-in is logged, click to retrieve it and access resources to support or elevate your mood. Then, take a moment to share your thoughts and resources below.

- What tools did the app suggest for you?
- Did you notice a recommended article for you to explore? If so, what are your thoughts on the recommendation?
- Do the definitions of your emotion(s) accurately describe your feelings or mood?
- Could this mobile application help you practice affect labeling regularly?

____

____

____

____

____

____

____

🔍 TIPS

- When you practice affect labeling regularly, it becomes automatic over time. The challenge is to remember to use this tool throughout your day. An effective way to start is to set a timer on your phone or calendar. When the timer goes off, label your emotions as accurately as possible.
- If you choose to use the *How We Feel* mobile application, you can schedule regular "check-ins." This is an excellent way to consistently practice affect labeling so that it becomes habitual.

Summary and Reflection

Self-awareness is the foundation upon which internal emotional intelligence skills rest. Without it, self-regulation and motivation remain reactive rather than deliberate.

Gratitude practices redirect neural pathways toward a positive mindset that naturally decreases negative thoughts and emotions. Expressive writing releases accumulated emotions, resulting in a sense of calm and clarity. Affect labeling creates distance between feelings and reactions by deliberately engaging cognition, which lessens reactivity. Each practice strengthens your capacity to recognize emotional states before they dictate your choices.

With each self-awareness practice, you are building an infrastructure so that neural patterns become more accessible each time you engage. Over weeks and months, you will find that what once required effort becomes reflexive. You will notice emotional shifts earlier, recover from stress faster, and respond to challenges with greater intention.

Before moving to self-regulation activities, work through the reflection activity provided so that you are clear on which tools align with your current needs and how you might integrate self-awareness strategies into your daily schedule.

- **When considering the three self-awareness tools and activities provided in this chapter: gratitude practices, expressive writing, and affect labeling, which tool(s) best fits your needs right now, and why?**

- **How will you integrate one of more of the tools and activities into your routine over the next two weeks?**

Chapter 3
Self-Regulation Activities

Self-regulation takes the emotional clarity developed through self-awareness and directs it toward effective action. Recognizing your stress response and what triggers it matters a great deal, but that recognition alone won't always stop you from reacting impulsively when a crisis erupts. Self-regulation tools give you techniques to calm your nervous system, interrupt automatic reactions, and access reasoning abilities that stress typically shuts down. These strategies enable you to lead with composure when circumstances intensify.

We will highlight techniques and activities for three highly effective self-regulation tools in the following pages:

✓ **Breathwork**: Techniques that promote intentional breathing to lower stress and enhance focus in the moment.

✓ **Cognitive Reframing**: Identifies negative thoughts and reframes them for accuracy. These practices activate clarity and a problem-solving mindset.

✓ **Grounding**: Directs attention and interrupts distressing emotions by anchoring you in the present moment.

Breathwork Practices

Breathwork involves the deliberate control of your breathing patterns. When you practice breathwork, your heart rate slows down, cortisol levels decrease, and your focus improves. Studies show that a brief daily breathwork practice (around five minutes) reduces anxiety and improves your mood.[1] Incorporating this tool into your daily routine gives you a practical method to regain composure quickly, making it valuable for educators who need to remain steady under pressure. As with all tools and strategies for inner harmony, breathwork requires consistent practice to become automatic in highly stressful moments.

Before exploring breathwork techniques, complete the exercise below to experience how simply becoming conscious of your breathing can affect your nervous system.

Conscious Breathing

Try this exercise!

- Simply notice your breathing as it is right now.
- Are you breathing quickly, or slowly?
- Is your breathing shallow, or deep?
- Breathe in fully, hold for five seconds, then exhale fully. Repeat this two more times.
- Now notice your breathing again. Has it changed?
- Do you notice a change in your level of balance or relaxation?

In *Transformational Tools for Special Educators* (Corwin, 2026), we outline the process for belly breathing, box breathing, alternate nostril breathing, and coherent breathing. These four practices are proven effective in reducing stress and anxiety and restoring a sense of balance and composure. Diaphragmatic or belly breathing and coherent slow breathing have the most consistent and well-developed research support, but alternate nostril breathing also has substantial supportive evidence, particularly within yoga research. Box breathing is used by first responders and military personnel, and it continues to be validated in more focused, modern trials.

Take some time to review the process for each method on the following page. Since breathwork exercises usually take about five to ten minutes, it would be most helpful to try them out in real-time while you review so that you can determine which practice works best for you. Then, complete the practice exercises that follow.

Breathwork Practices

Belly Breathing

- Sit or lie down in a comfortable position.
- Place one hand on your chest, and the other on your abdomen.
- Inhale deeply through your nose, allowing your belly to fully expand and pause briefly.
- Exhale slowly through your mouth, contracting your abdominal muscles to expel as much air as possible.
- Repeat for three to five minutes.

Coherent Breathing

- Find a comfortable seated or lying position.
- Inhale slowly and deeply through your nose for six seconds, allowing your belly to expand.
- Without pausing, exhale slowly through your nose or mouth for a count of six seconds.
- Try to create a balanced breathing pattern that focuses on smooth transitions between inhaling and exhaling.
- Maintain this breathing pattern for three to five minutes.

Alternate Nostril Breathing

- Sit comfortably with your spine straight.
- Using your right thumb, gently close your right nostril.
- Inhale slowly and deeply through your left nostril. At the peak of this inhale, close your left nostril with your right and pinky fingers while simultaneously releasing your right nostril.
- Exhale slowly through the right nostril, pause, and then inhale through the right nostril, close it with your thumb, and exhale through the left nostril.
- This completes one cycle. Five cycles are usually recommended for optimal results.

Box Breathing

- Stand or sit in a comfortable position. Your spine should be straight, and your muscles relaxed.
- Inhale slowly through your nose for a count of four, filling your lungs completely.
- Hold your breath for a count of four.
- Exhale gently and completely through your mouth for a count of four.
- Pause, and count to four before beginning another cycle.

Breathwork Micro Practice

The value of integrating breathwork throughout your day is best discovered by allowing yourself a full week of practice, followed by analysis and reflection. The following framework is an excellent way to get started.

- Choose one to two preferred breathwork techniques.
- Identify three or four short windows in your day when practicing breathwork is realistic. This might be a few minutes before students or staff arrive, just before lunch, or as you transition between meetings or classes.
- Write down each time window and the specific breathing technique you will use during that time. You can choose one practice, like belly breathing, or you can combine techniques and start with belly breathing, then end your session with alternate nostril breathing. Choose the techniques that work best for YOU.
- Decide how long you will practice (usually between three and five minutes), or how many breathwork cycles you will complete.
- Set a reminder, such as a phone alarm or calendar alert, so you do not have to rely on memory.

Commit to following the framework for a week. Then, at the end of the week, review your experience by answering the following questions in the space provided. Remember that you can adjust your practice to best fit your needs.

1. Did you practice your chosen method(s) consistently all week?
2. What changes did you notice in your body, mood, or focus?
3. Were there any barriers that made it harder to follow through with your practice? If so, what were they?

____

____

____

____

____

____

____

Cognitive Reframing

Cognitive reframing helps reduce stress and conflict by shifting reactive assumptions to thoughtful discernment. In practice, it asks you to slow down and analyze your first reaction by noticing the automatic thought that appears, examining whether the thought is accurate or helpful, then replacing your initial thought with a more balanced, realistic, and constructive interpretation.

When you return to this practice regularly, your brain begins to favor these more realistic appraisals, and your emotions become easier to manage in the moment. Over time, you strengthen neural pathways that support thinking before acting or reacting. Stressful experiences become sources of insight and strength rather than events that drain your energy. This shift allows you to stay grounded, think clearly, and remain effective, even in the most demanding environments.

Before reviewing cognitive reframing strategies and completing the associated exercise, take a moment to complete the short *Thoughts Check* below.

If you answered "yes" to question one or two, cognitive reframing provides a way to transform negative, unhelpful thoughts into more neutral interpretations so that you can remain regulated and move forward from a place of balance and clarity. If you answered "no" to questions one and two, then you may already engage in cognitive reframing or other methods that favor thinking through a challenge prior to taking action. In this case, the techniques provided here can enhance your current practice or give you new methods to consider.

Cognitive Reframing

Socratic Questioning

When a negative thought arises, either suddenly or in response to an event, Socratic questioning invites you to pause and investigate it by asking:

1) What evidence supports this thought?
2) What evidence contradicts it?
3) Am I assuming the worst outcome?
4) How would I advise a colleague or friend having the same thought?

Moving through these questions shifts you away from a purely emotional reaction and activates your thinking brain, creating space for a more balanced and accurate interpretation.

Cognitive Distancing

Cognitive distancing is a powerful and easy way to remember that your thoughts are mental events, not unquestionable facts. When a harsh or discouraging thought arises about yourself or others, you pause, notice it, and examine it from a neutral vantage point.

For example, instead of thinking, "I will never be able to learn French," you might stop, step back, and reframe it as, "I am finding French difficult right now, and I may benefit from one to one tutoring to enhance my learning and move forward."

Perspective Shifting

Perspective shifting is especially useful when you find yourself assigning a negative meaning to a personal or professional interaction. Instead of treating your first interpretation as the truth, you intentionally explore alternative viewpoints, asking what else might explain the same situation or event.

For example, if your colleague sighs and walks away from you unexpectedly, you might assume she is angry with you. When you shift perspectives and imagine the situation from her position, you might recall that she has not been sleeping well and may be exhausted rather than upset. This opens space for curiosity instead of certainty, allowing you to approach your co-worker with a more open, grounded mindset.

When you use cognitive reframing methods consistently, your thoughts will begin to shift automatically. Your responses start to come from a place of composure and curiosity, and staying regulated amidst negative encounters becomes your default.

The example below illustrates how the cognitive reframing technique, Socratic Questioning, effectively challenges initial assumptions and replaces them with a more realistic and constructive mindset.

Example Scenario: *An English teacher tutored a student for several months to prepare him for his final exam in English Literature. He barely passes the final exam. Upon hearing the news, the teacher has two primary thoughts: "I failed this student," and "I wasted months of my time for nothing."*

Cognitive Reframe:

Using Socratic questioning, the teacher recognizes these thoughts and moves through selected steps of the process.

STEP ONE: Examine the evidence that supports and contradicts her initial thoughts

While the student's low grade on the final supports her initial thoughts, the teacher recalls that the student demonstrated progress during his sessions with her. Evidence includes significant improvements on quizzes, assignments, and general content knowledge. Clearly, learning and progress took place. This evidence contradicts the thought that she wasted her time and failed the student because he grew academically under her tutelage. Furthermore, one test grade alone is not enough evidence to support her initial thoughts, especially when considering all of the contradicting data.

STEP TWO: Respond to her thoughts the same way she would respond to a colleague in the same situation

If the teacher were advising a colleague in this situation, she would likely point out that a low test score can stem from many factors, such as test anxiety, lack of sleep, confusion about how the questions were written, or even self-sabotage. Assuming that the student's low test score was directly related to her competency alone is not realistic.

This short process allows the teacher to shift her thinking and approach the student with curiosity and support, exploring what may have interfered with the exam and how she might adjust her instruction to include test-taking strategies in the future.

▶ PRACTICE

Think about a recent event or interaction that triggered negative thoughts about yourself or others. Common examples include scenarios like:

- An educational leader assigns a task and a deadline. 50% of staff members don't meet the deadline. *Thought:* They don't respect me as a leader.
- A parent sends a threatening email. *Thought:* The parent disrespects me.
- A teacher spends hours working on an engaging instructional unit. Students are less engaged than before. *Thought:* I've wasted my time for nothing.

In the space below, write down the event, your thought(s), and use one of the cognitive reframing tools to reframe it. If you can't think of a personal example, use one of the scenarios provided.

____

____

____

____

____

____

____

The power of cognitive reframing rests in choosing a realistic interpretation of an event, then responding with intention rather than reacting defensively to untested assumptions. When situations are consistently approached through this lens, emotional responses become more regulated, reducing the intensity of stress, frustration, and overwhelm.

Grounding

Grounding practices are brief, practical tools that help you reconnect with what is happening right now. Instead of getting swept up in racing thoughts or rising emotions, grounding invites you to look around you, notice what your body feels, and pay attention to concrete details in your environment. Where cognitive reframing works with the story you are telling yourself, grounding gives your nervous system something steady and immediate to hold on to so that emotions can settle.

Sensory grounding centers on what you can see, hear, feel, smell, or taste in the moment. You might notice the texture of an object in your hand, the weight of your body in the chair, the pattern of sounds in the room, or a specific scent. When you deliberately tune in to several senses, the brain shifts away from stress responses and begins to move toward regulation. This kind of sensory focus can soften the intensity of distress and help you feel more anchored in the present.

Cognitive grounding uses simple mental tasks to give your mind a clear, structured focus. You might quietly name objects in the room, list categories or facts, describe the colors you see, or repeat a neutral, steadying phrase. These small tasks call on the parts of the brain that handle planning and problem solving, which can interrupt spiraling thoughts and make space for a calmer response.

The grounding techniques presented in *Transformational Tools for Special Educators* (Corwin, 2026) are summarized on the following page, and the associated practice activities will provide the opportunity for you to try them out in real time. Before moving forward, complete the short *Stress Check* below to get a better understanding of what stress looks like for you.

Most educators answer "yes" to questions one and/or two. If you already use a tool to reorient yourself, grounding can serve as an additional option to quickly reduce stress, anxiety, or overwhelm. If you do not use a tool or strategy when these feelings take hold, then using one of the grounding techniques provided is an excellent starting point.

Grounding Practices

5-4-3-2-1

Pause, and identify five things that you can see, four things you can touch, three things you can hear, two things you can smell, and one thing you can taste. This short exercise can be repeated until you feel a sense of calm.

Feet on the Floor

- Sit or stand in a comfortable position.
- Place your feet firmly on the floor.
- Slowly press your feet steadily into the ground while resting your attention on how your body feels.
- Maintain deliberate pressure, and allow your breathing to slow down.
- Note: This practice is suitable for the workplace, but if you have the option of moving outdoors and taking off your shoes, you will find this exercise even more effective.

Grounding Objects

Keep an textured object that you like close at hand. This could be a stress ball, fabric, a stone, or anything that is textured and can fit into your hand.

When stress or anxiety spikes, hold the object and take a moment to focus on your object's detail. Notice the object's temperature, weight, contours, etc. Let yourself be completely focused and immersed in the object and the sensations you feel from handling it.

Verbal Grounding

Begin by taking a breath and stating clear, simple facts to anchor yourself into the present moment. An example might be, "I am sitting comfortably in my chair." Try to engage all of your senses by including what you can hear, smell, and feel: "My back feels warm against the chair. The leather is smooth and I feel cool air on my face."

Choose two grounding tools and give them a try right now. After each one, answer the following questions in the space provided.

1. Which technique did you choose?
2. After completing the practice, how do you feel? Do you notice a sense of calmness, centeredness? If not, do you notice any shift at all?
3. Did you find it difficult to engage with grounding exercises? If so, what made it challenging?

Grounding is a deceptively simple practice that yields notable results quickly. By bringing your attention to the present moment in the midst of a crisis or stressful encounter, reactivity is interrupted, allowing your emotions to regulate and reset in real time.

- It is important to engage fully in the present when using grounding techniques. If you get distracted or find yourself rushing through the process, restart with the intention to focus only on the practice.
- Should you not feel regulated right away, repeat your chosen technique until a sense of calm takes hold.

Summary and Reflection

Cultivating insight into your emotions is important, but in the middle of a conflict or crisis, insight alone rarely keeps you from snapping, shutting down, or absorbing more than your system can hold. Self-regulation tools give your body and brain a sequence to follow when pressure rises. Breathwork slows physiological arousal so that your nervous system can step back from survival mode. Cognitive reframing steadies your thinking so that you can interpret events more accurately and respond from a place of measured clarity. Grounding allows you to regain composure by bringing your attention into the present moment so that your emotions can settle.

With regular practice, these strategies begin to shape your automatic patterns. You will notice stress and emotional escalation sooner, shift from reactivity to choice more quickly, and return to a workable level of calm after difficult encounters. Over time, you are not only recovering from stress but also leading with a steadier presence that supports students, families, and colleagues.

Before moving into the next chapter, take a few minutes to complete the reflection activity and identify which self-regulation tools you intend to lean on most in your current environment.

- Think about the activities related to the three self-regulation tools presented in this chapter: breathwork, cognitive reframing, and grounding. Choose two activities that stood out for you, and write down how and why these activities come to mind.

- How would you describe the difference between self-awareness and self-regulation tools?

- Will you integrate one or more self-regulation strategy into your daily routine? If so, which ones? If not, why not?

Chapter 4
Motivation Activities

When people talk about motivation, they often use words like willpower or discipline. Some will say motivation is a mood that includes feelings of confidence or optimism, while others may perceive it as a burst of energy that comes through inspiration. There is some truth in these answers, but motivation can best be understood as a complex system that gives you the energy to engage, a clear sense of direction, and the resilience to stay the course.[1] From an emotional intelligence perspective, motivation can relate to endurance. "It is the quiet force that propels you forward even when the path seems steep and uncertain."[2]

When motivation is viewed as a psychological system and not something that just "happens," you gain leverage over it. You are no longer waiting to feel motivated. Instead, you learn to deliberately shape the conditions that activate your inner drive when pressure is high and energy is limited. When motivation is developed alongside self-awareness and self-regulation, these capacities function together as a dynamic triad, allowing you to move forward despite obstacles or external stressors.

The human experience involves both external and internal motivation. When motivated externally, you are working for the payoff or reward, and this works well when you need a push to get started. Internal motivation is notably different:

> While external motivation depends on outside rewards, such as recognition, monetary incentives, or praise, internal motivation stems from passion, a sense of purpose, and the satisfaction derived from mastering challenges.[3]

Both types of motivation have their place, but when developing emotional intelligence skills, the focus is almost always on internal motivation, because this is what drives you through long-term challenges and fosters resilience.

In Transformational Tools for Special Educators (Corwin, 2026), we shared three tools to develop internal motivation, and we will focus on each of these here:

✓ **Intrinsic Goal Setting**: Setting goals driven by personal fulfillment, curiosity, and growth.

✓ **Self-Efficacy**: Rooted in Social Cognitive Theory and works to build trust in the ability to overcome challenges.

✓ **Mindset Development**: Based on Growth Mindset Theory and cultivates a mindset where challenges become opportunities.

Intrinsic Goal Setting

Intrinsic goal setting aligns your goals with what matters most to you. This alignment makes every task inherently meaningful, and the drive to keep moving forward occurs naturally and is sustained over time.

This practice can be applied to goals that you set for yourself or goals that are externally assigned by your supervisor, school, or district. In either case, the first step is to fully understand your personal values or what drives you at your deepest levels.

To gain deeper insight into what matters most to you, choose and complete one or more of the practice exercises below, then write down three to five of your core values.

⏩ PRACTICE

- Reflect on peak moments in your life - the times when you felt proud, fulfilled, or deeply at peace. Notice what values were present in those moments. This could be something like integrity, creativity, or achievement.
- Write about what frustrates or angers you most in daily life or society. Strong emotional reactions often signal a violated value.
- Visualize your ideal day. Imagine where you are, what you are doing, and who you are with. Consider any themes that emerge, like connection,

growth, freedom, or something else. These themes can often reveal what you care about.

- Utilize an online option that offers activities or prompts to assess your values. *The Acceptance and Commitment Therapy Values Card Sort* is a great option. It is free, easy to use, and prompts consideration of values that you feel are very important, important, or not important.

After completing one or more of the above activities, answer the following questions:

1. What core values did you discover?
2. Did the exercises uncover any values that you were not previously aware of?

____

____

____

____

____

____

____

With a clear understanding of what really matters to you, the next step is to either set goals that align closely with your values or align externally assigned goals with your personal values. A few examples of values and aligned goals are provided.

VALUE: **Independence**

A teacher sets an intrinsic goal to build a business that will provide a secondary income and holds the potential to become his primary income.

VALUE: **Helping Others**

A social worker sets her intrinsic goal to pursue a license in clinical social work. This will expand her skills and knowledge, increasing the number of people she can positively impact.

VALUE: **Professional Growth**

A special education assistant director is directed to develop a detailed strategic plan for her program. Even though this is a daunting task, she is able to recognize its internal alignment with her value to grow professionally. Professional growth becomes her motivation to commit to the task.

VALUE: **Collaboration and Creativity**

A teacher leader is assigned to a team of peers and tasked with creating a major section of the district's new curriculum. The project is formidable, but she finds internal alignment with two of her key values. The collaborative nature of the task and the creative nature of the project support her motivation to engage.

Setting personal or professional goals that directly relate to your values is relatively straightforward. However, when you first begin aligning external goals to your priorities, it can be a challenging task. However, with consistent reflection, it is usually possible to identify some meaningful connections between external expectations and what you are passionate about. Even when full alignment is not achievable, elements of a task can often be reframed in ways that hold personal significance.

Two intrinsic goal-setting examples are provided below, followed by opportunities for you to directly apply this tool.

Example One: Intrinsic Goal Setting

Scenario: *An administrator is clear on her personal values and priorities. At the beginning of the school year, she sets the following value-aligned goal to sustain her motivation throughout the year.*

Value: Supporting and encouraging others

Goal: As a ninth-grade administrator, I will work to create an environment that feels safe, supportive, and positive for my team.

Action Plan:

- Check-ins two times weekly with two to four staff members. I will spend 15 minutes with each person, asking how things are going and what I can do to support. I will add tasks to support to my to-do list and follow up.
- Twice a day, I will set my timer and personally give specific praise to at least one staff member. This can be through text, email, or in person.
- I will arrange a 25-minute coffee chat one morning each week, which is not mandatory. For those who attend, we will each share "one positive thing" for the week and discuss ways that we can all support the ninth-grade team.

Example Two: Aligned Intrinsic Goal Setting

Scenario: *A veteran teacher is assigned to mentor a new teacher. Initially, the additional work is concerning as she has little to no extra time during the day. When considering this task and how it might relate to her values, she discovers:*

- She values growth and advancement at this stage of her career. One of her long-term goals is to move into leadership, and she values leadership that deeply supports teachers and support staff.
- As a new teacher mentor, she can discover some of the challenges new teachers face. She can then create potential solutions to these challenges and share insights with the leadership team. This shows her readiness to advance.

Viewing this task as aligned with her values and long-term goal, the teacher naturally becomes internally motivated to do it. She finds creative ways to delegate some of her tasks so that she has enough time to support both the new teacher and herself.

PRACTICE

Exercise One: *Set an Intrinsic Goal*

With your core values in mind, set a professional goal that is directly linked to one of your key priorities. Note your value, your goal, and your action plan.

Many educators share goals like *making a positive difference* or *helping students discover the importance of literature, math, science, etc.* But educators may also value *personal growth and achievement, creating a positive classroom environment,* or *creating an inclusive school culture.* No value is really better or more acceptable than another. What matters is being very clear on what matters to YOU.

____

____

____

____

____

____

____

Exercise Two: *Align an Assigned Goal or Task*

Choose a current or recent task or goal that was assigned to you. If you can't think of one, an example scenario is provided. Carefully consider any aspect that you might link to one or more of your core values.

Example Scenario: *You have been tasked with providing a series of training sessions on best practices for multisensory learning.*

____

____

____

____

____

____

____

Once you begin setting goals and aligning tasks in this way, your work can become a source of genuine engagement fueled by moments of inspiration.

Self Efficacy

Consider your personal skill set. Are there things that you do very well? If so, what are they? Those are the areas that already carry a quiet sense of confidence for you. You know that if you show up and do what you know how to do, you can handle any task related to your expertise.

Developing self-efficacy means extending that same grounded trust into areas that still feel difficult or unfamiliar, where success is not automatic, and confidence has to be built over time. You probably did not arrive at your current strengths by accident. You might have watched others who were already skilled, separated the larger task into smaller steps, integrated feedback from colleagues or supervisors, or practiced until the process felt more natural. Even if you are naturally good at something, expertise usually develops over time.

Consider a special educator who has long struggled to manage severe behavior escalations in the classroom. She recognizes that her training did not adequately prepare her to manage random outbursts or prolonged disruption. Although the process feels awkward at first, she commits to learning a new response protocol. She studies the steps, rehearses them deliberately, writes a brief script she can recall under pressure, and practices her tone and body posture.

During a challenging incident, she follows the plan closely. The student who typically escalates and triggers the class returns to calm more quickly than usual, and the rest of the class settles sooner than in previous episodes. For the first time, she experiences a glimpse of potential mastery. Later, while reviewing a video of a colleague managing a similar situation, she notices that her own pacing, distance, and language closely mirror what she observes. Each of these experiences contributes to a growing, evidence-based belief that she can develop the skills needed to manage behavior crises effectively. This belief, strengthened through continued practice and reinforcement, reflects self-efficacy development in action.

Take a moment to complete the short exercise below before reviewing the techniques aligned with self-efficacy development on the following page.

1. At the beginning of this section, you were asked to think about the things that you do well. Write down a few of these skills in the space provided.
2. Choose one or two items from your list and reflect on how you developed efficacy in those skills. Was it practice? Feedback? Were you "naturally" good at it? List these items next to the skill(s) you chose.

____

____

____

____

____

____

____

Most people find that even if they have a natural ability in things like project management, leadership, music, or sports, efficacy is not developed from ability alone. Those who excel usually practice regularly, celebrate their progress, and may even study others who are successful to find new ways to improve. Many also use visualization techniques to cultivate self-efficacy. The techniques that follow offer a few research-based ways to build efficacy so that you can approach challenges with optimism and sustained motivation.

Self-Efficacy Practices

Visualization

There are two primary types of visualization used for internal motivation: outcome and mental rehearsal. Each is effective at increasing your confidence, and both provide a "push" to get started.

Outcome Visualization:
When you vividly imagine a desired outcome, whether it is a specific goal, a change in yourself, or shift in your environment, the emotional charge of that image gives you a "boost" to begin and a feeling that you can make it happen.

Technique: Visualize your outcome with as much detail as possible. Imagine the physical sensations you might feel, the mental relief of success, and the positive feelings of completion. Are you celebrating? Relaxing?

Process Visualization:
The emphasis on what you will do, rather than the outcome, creates a clear mental script of the steps needed to achieve your desire(s).

Technique: Visualize yourself moving through the steps that lead to your end-goal. Picture the setting where you will begin, the materials or tools you will use, and the sequence of actions you will take. What does the very first step look like? How do you move from one step to the next?

Self-Monitoring

Self-monitoring involves regularly assessing your progress, evaluating your strategies, and making adjustments to maintain alignment with personal goals.

-Begin by setting aside dedicated time each week for self-reflection.

-Use a journal or a structured template to document what went well, what challenges arose, and how they were managed.

-Ask specific questions like, "What strategies helped me succeed?" and "How can I apply this learning to future challenges?"

When setbacks occur, view them as opportunities to learn and refine your approach. This method not only builds self-efficacy but also helps maintain motivation!

Consider a task or skill that you would like to master. Using both types of visualization, complete the following activity.

Visualization Activity

- Visualize yourself successfully completing the task, or imagine yourself demonstrating the skill. Include as many details as you can. How do you feel? What does your mastery look like? What are people saying about your efficacy? How are people or the environment changed because of your contribution(s)?
- Now think about how you might start learning the skill or begin the task. Picture yourself moving easily through each step of the process. Imagine the vivid details of each step, and see yourself engaging effortlessly, moving past any obstacles you may encounter.

Based on your process visualization, write down your plan of action below. Be sure to include a self-monitoring activity described on page 43.

____

____

____

____

____

____

____

Expectations, duties, and tasks can shift rapidly in the field of education. When responsibilities fall outside your strengths or your training, frustration and overwhelm are natural responses. But when you choose to intentionally build self-efficacy in these moments, uncertainty becomes a starting point for growth and a catalyst to build resilience.

Mindset Development

Obstacles have a way of quietly undermining motivation. When effort repeatedly meets resistance, it becomes harder to sustain forward momentum, even when the goal still matters. Developing a growth mindset enhances your internal motivation by helping you stay engaged, optimistic, and persistent when facing barriers. When you choose to perceive challenges as opportunities, you begin to shift into a state of positivity that bolsters your belief that, regardless of the obstacles, success is achievable.

Process-oriented goal setting reinforces a way of thinking and planning that aligns with growth mindset practices. Before you review the steps of process-oriented goal setting and complete the associated activity, take a moment to answer the following questions.

Goals Check
Circle the Best Answer.

1) Have you engaged in goal setting personally, or professionally?
   Yes   No

2) If you answered "Yes" to question one, what is the typical outcome of your goal setting practices?
   Always meet goal(s)   Sometimes meet goal(s)   Rarely meet goal(s)

3) If you answered "No" to question one, do you feel that goal setting could be a helpful practice for you personally or professionally?
   Yes   No   Maybe

Regardless of your experience or success with goal setting, using a process-oriented technique will support both initial and ongoing engagement with your desired result. Process-oriented goal setting breaks big objectives into consistent, repeatable actions that are positioned in the present. Instead of concentrating only on the end result: a completed dissertation, a marathon medal, or a published book, you emphasize the daily behaviors that make your achievement possible. For instance, committing to write for forty minutes every morning, running three days a week, or drafting one section of a chapter per work session are all process-oriented goals.

The shift from *outcome* to *process* matters because outcomes are often distant, uncertain, or outside your full control, but processes are concrete and immediately actionable.

Process-Oriented Goal Setting

☑   Break your large goal into small steps that are relatively easy to complete. For example, if you are creating a training program, choose a process goal of completing one activity or section per day. Make sure the action is something that you can complete in one sitting on a regular basis. It is perfectly fine to complete more than one section of the training program if you have time, but your process goal should not change - it should remain a small, achievable action.

☑   Keep a checklist or data sheet so that you can mark each time that you complete the process goal, and plan to review your data on a regular basis. Reviews can be weekly, biweekly, or monthly - frequency is not as important as consistency.

☑   During your data reviews, pay close attention to the days when your process goal was not completed. Consider the setting, timing, or situational variables that interfered, then compare those conditions with the days when you met your goal. If patterns emerge, take special notice of them so that you can adjust accordingly. You may notice, for example, that success occurred when you started first thing in the morning, while postponing the task until later in the day led to missing your goal. Making a minor adjustment to complete your activity or section first thing will keep you on track.

☑   At the end of your data reviews, celebrate your accomplishments! Even if you do not meet your goal consistently, give yourself credit for all of the days when you DID complete your goal. If data shows that you met your goal four times out of seven, focus on the face that you successfully completed four sections or activities that might have not been completed without your goal in place!

Think about some things that you would like to change, and choose one that is at
the top of your priority list. This can be as simple as eating more vegetables or more
aspirational, like exercising five times a week or creating an online learning
program. Once you have a clear outcome in mind, follow the steps provided to form
your process goal. Refer to the sequential steps on the previous page to be sure you
include all of the necessary components.

- Consider how your outcome can be broken down into small parts or steps.
  What things need to be done for you to reach your end result? Be sure that
  each step can be completed easily, and write down your process steps in
  the space provided.
- Write down how you will keep data on the small step (or steps) you have
  chosen. This can be a simple checklist, a spreadsheet, or a mobile app. The
  key is to keep it simple and remember that you are only recording whether
  you completed your small step or not.
- Choose how often you will review your data. This is totally up to you, but
  give yourself at least three or four days before assessing. Write down how
  often you will review in the space below, and note that you will adjust your
  process goal if you are not consistently meeting it. Also, note that you will
  celebrate the days that you completed the task because every completion is
  one step closer to your desired outcome!

____

____

____

____

____

____

____

- Try not to think too much about the final outcome as you work through your process goals. The best results come from keeping your thoughts on meeting the associated small steps that will eventually lead to your desired result.
- Readjusting your process goal based on your data is crucial. For example, if you intend to write one page each day in order to complete a novel, but your tracking shows that this happens only three out of seven days, reflection becomes necessary. Paying attention to what occurs on the days when writing does not happen often reveals patterns. If you notice that checking email first leads to distraction and derails the writing session, the adjustment is straightforward, and the goal is augmented to include that writing must happen before engaging in any other activity, including email.
- Celebrating your success is also imperative. In the example above, even though the full seven days of writing were not achieved, three pages were completed, which still brings you closer to your ultimate goal.

Summary and Reflection

When you master self-awareness and self-regulation, you gain the capacity to notice stress, frustration, and overwhelm as they arise, rather than being overtaken by them. This awareness creates space for you to self-regulate in ways that support you and others more effectively.

Mastery of your inner drive, or intrinsic motivation, anchors awareness and regulation to purpose and growth. Motivation provides the energy and direction needed to apply self-awareness and self-regulation strategies consistently, especially during moments of challenge or fatigue.

Intrinsic goal-setting ensures that your tasks or goals actually matter to you, personally. This moves you forward naturally, because engagement feels easier when your actions align with your purpose. Self-efficacy practices transform doubt or overwhelm into possibility, and Mindset Development shifts your perception of challenges and obstacles into opportunities for success.

When considering the internal domains of emotional intelligence:

> The internal domains work in harmony, each reinforcing the others in a balanced, purposeful way. When used together, these tools create a powerful process of reflection and meaningful action. Self-awareness provides the foundation for recognizing emotions and identifying thought patterns, and self-regulation ensures that those insights translate into intentional, adaptive responses. Internal motivation supports this process by fueling the ongoing drive for growth and resilience. [4]

Next, we will explore practices that target the external domains of emotional intelligence: empathy and social skills. Before moving forward, take a moment to review the three internal skills covered in Part One, and complete the Reflection Activity that follows.

- Now that you have explored and practiced intrinsic goal setting, self-efficacy, and process-oriented goal setting, which practice appealed to you the most and why?

- Do you think that cultivating intrinsic motivation will make a difference in your levels of stress, overwhelm, or frustration? If so, how? If not, why not?

- Write down your key values or what matters most to you, and briefly explain why you consider these values a top priority.

Part Two

External Mastery

Creating the Culture

Chapter 5
Introduction to External Skills

The process of becoming your best self, or the best at what you do may begin with internal mastery, but this is definitely not where the impact of your effort ends. Once you strenghten your internal emotional intelligence skills, they begin to show up in the places that matter most: in conversations, collaboration, conflict, and repair. External skills are the visible expression of your inner mastery.

In Chapter One, we positioned internal mastery as the roots of a tree or the foundation upon which external skills are built. External skills are the tree's trunk and branches that allow your inner stability to translate into connection, influence, and shared problem-solving.

The next two chapters focus on empathy and social skills, in accordance with the last two emotional intelligence domains. Empathy is the capacity to sense what may be happening in another person and communicate in a way that lowers threat and increases trust. It is not necessarily agreement, nor is it absorbing someone else's emotions. It is the practice of seeing clearly, listening beneath the surface, and responding with accuracy and respect. Social skills build on that attunement, moving empathy into effective interaction. These are the tools that help you communicate with clarity, set boundaries with steadiness, and navigate difficult conversations without escalation.

It is essential to remember that your outward skills are inseparable from what is happening internally. The way you communicate, empathize, and engage with others is shaped by your level of self-awareness, your capacity for self-regulation, and the strength of your internal motivation. When these internal systems are strained or underdeveloped, even well-intended communication can sound abrupt or misaligned. Your nervous system influences the tone, pacing, and timing of every interaction. If you lack self-awareness or regulation, then under elevated stress, responses are more likely to be reactive rather than intentional. When your internal skills are developed, you are better able to pause, modulate your tone, and respond with clarity even in challenging moments.

In the chapters that follow, we introduce empathy tools first, because connection is the gateway to collaboration. Next, we present selected social skills tools because effective relationships require both warmth and structure. As your skills build through the activities that follow, they become a steady way of engaging with others. This allows you to contribute to a culture defined by healthy boundaries, trust, responsiveness, productive collaboration, and meaningful connection.

Chapter 6
Empathy Activities

In educational settings shaped by stress and high emotional demands, empathy plays a critical role in building trust and creating conditions where individuals feel seen and valued. When practiced deliberately, empathy influences how others perceive behavior, interpret emotional cues, and respond.

Many people think of empathy as the ability to understand and share another person's feelings, and while this is true, empathy is more than that. It can be better understood as an intentional process rather than a passive ability. People are often described as naturally empathetic or, conversely, emotionally detached or indifferent. Empathy, however, is not a fixed personality trait. Your brain adapts to repeated patterns of thought and behavior, so empathic responses can be learned and strengthened with consistent practice.

We will focus on two powerful empathy tools here:

✓ **Perspective-Taking Exercises:** Engages the brain's mirror neurons and promote cognitive flexibility so that listeners avoid assumptions.

✓ **Trauma-Informed Empathy:** Views behavior as communication and increases empathy and effective interventions because behavior is understood as a response to traumatic events.

Perspective-Taking Exercises

When you make a concerted effort to imagine a situation from another's point of view, you cultivate empathy and cognitive flexibility. Instead of making assumptions that may or may not be true, you begin to foster insight and understanding, which strengthens connections and reduces conflict. [1]

Most educators have encountered the practice of perspective-taking through professional development sessions and best practices training. However, when demands increase and deadlines approach, it is easy to lose sight of this mindset. The good news is, the more you practice perspective-taking, the more automatic it becomes, even during intense, stressful circumstances.

Before reviewing three ways to engage in perspective-taking, answer the questions below.

Perspective Check

Circle the Best Answer.

1) When a person who seems angry or frustrated confronts you, how do you typically feel?

   I feel attacked | I feel uncomfortable | I feel curious | I feel something else

2) How often do you think about a situation from another person's point of view?

   Never   Sometimes   Often   Very Often

3) Have you ever felt like a person's behavior was directed towards you (personally), then later discovered the behavior was related to something else?

   Yes   No   Not Sure

Question one of the *Perspective Check* is particularly relevant for educators who regularly encounter angry parents, students, or colleagues. These confrontations can feel deeply personal, particularly if your work is directly challenged.

Perspective-taking is not about taking the high road or suppressing frustration that may be justified. It is about considering what might be driving the other person's behavior so you can respond deliberately rather than react defensively. The following example illustrates the difference.

- *A parent emails you demanding to know why their child failed a recent assignment, insinuating that this was somehow your fault.*

Reacting: You fire back an email defending your grading criteria and pointing out that the student didn't study or follow directions. The parent escalates her complaint to administration.

Responding: You pause and consider: this parent might be anxious about their child's overall progress, embarrassed by the grade, or feeling pressure from the student. You respond by acknowledging their concern, offering specific feedback about what the student struggled with, and suggesting concrete next steps. The parent feels heard, the student gets support, and the situation de-escalates.

The "responding" example is not always easy in situations like these, but the more you practice perspective-taking, the more it will become your go-to response.

Read through the different ways you can engage with this practice, and complete the activity that follows.

Perspective-Taking

The following practices can help you imagine any situation from a different point of view, which will encourage you to respond with empathy.

Role Reversal

Role reversal involves imagining yourself in another person's situation, considering their feelings, experiences, and challenges.

This practice encourages responses rooted in curiosity and understanding rather than frustration.

- Imagine the situation from the other person's perspective by asking what pressures, needs, or past experiences might be shaping their response right now.
- Identify what the person may be feeling beneath the behavior, even if that feeling is not being expressed clearly or appropriately.
- Consider how the situation might look if you had the same constraints, history, or emotional load.

Visualization

This practice simply requires you to take a moment and visualize a situation from another person's point of view. Visualization only takes a few minutes and can quickly shift your response to others.

Practice by closing your eyes and imagining the situation from the other person's point of view. Envision their surroundings, the stressors they might face, their history, and how they might interpret the situation.

Guided Reflection

Structured reflection helps shift thinking away from immediate emotional reactions and toward a broader, more compassionate perspective. Ask yourself prompts such as:

- If I were in their position, what emotions might I be experiencing?
- What external factors might influence their behavior?
- What need or concern is this person's behavior attempting to communicate?

Our instinct under pressure is self-protection, not understanding. This is why perspective-taking does not come naturally in moments of stress or conflict. It is a skill that truly requires deliberate, consistent practice.

A scenario is provided below. Read carefully, and answer the associated questions in the space provided.

Scenario: You are a World History teacher, and the school counselor asks to meet with you. She shares that one of your high school students has accused you of not liking him and yelling at him all of the time. Neither of these accusations is true, yet the counselor asks you to commit to an online training that focuses on sensitivity and empathy.

- What might be the student's perspective?
- The counselor seems to be assuming the student is truthful. What is her perspective?
- Given both points of view, what will your response to the counselor be, and what, if anything, will you do about how the student feels?

____

____

____

____

____

____

____

Perspective taking does not require you to excuse bad behavior or abandon your professional boundaries. It is a practice that creates just enough internal space to respond with clarity, intention, and emotional steadiness when situations feel charged. If you regularly practice this skill, you can remain grounded in your values under pressure while building stronger relationships and reducing unnecessary conflicts.

Trauma-Informed Empathy

If you are an educator, then you work regularly with students who have special needs. If you are a special educator, you serve this population as your primary focus. Given the elevated trauma exposure for students receiving special services, developing trauma-informed empathy is not optional. It is an essential skill that helps you respond effectively to student crises.

Students with disabilities experience trauma at disproportionately high rates. Research shows they are twice as likely to face abuse and neglect when compared to peers without disabilities.[2] Students with emotional and behavioral disorders show particularly elevated trauma exposure. One study showed that 96.4% experienced at least one adverse childhood experience, and over half (59.9%) experienced four or more adverse experiences.[3]

The elevated trauma exposure among students with special needs has profound implications for educational practice, as trauma significantly impacts attention, memory, self-regulation, and the foundational capacities necessary for learning.[4]

While these statistics highlight the urgent need for trauma-informed approaches in special education, trauma is not exclusive to students with disabilities. General education students also experience adverse childhood experiences at significant rates, so trauma affects learners across all classroom settings.

Students who have experienced trauma often communicate distress through behaviors that can disrupt the classroom, or sometimes, the entire school. When educators interpret these behaviors as defiance rather than as stress responses, interventions tend to fail, and discipline escalates.

Trauma-informed empathy shifts the conversation from *"**What is wrong with this person?**"* to *"**What happened to this person?**"* This is an important shift because it reframes behavior as a response to experience rather than a reflection of character. When educators recognize challenging behavior as trauma-driven communication, they can respond more effectively. In doing so, students show measurable improvement.[5]

Complete the short exercise below to gain insight into how you connect trauma with behavior, then explore the four themes that can help you develop trauma-informed empathy.

Trauma Knowledge Check

Circle the Best Answer.

1) Before reading this section, were you aware that students with disabilities experience trauma at significantly higher rates than their peers?

   Yes   No   Somewhat

2) When you encounter challenging student behavior, do you usually consider whether trauma might be a factor?

   Never   Sometimes   Often   Very Often

3) When thinking about the challenging students you work with, could traumatic experiences explain some of their behavior ?

   Yes   No   Not Sure

While trauma-informed empathy is not a formally recognized clinical term, it is introduced in *Transformational Tools for Special Educators* (Corwin, 2026) to reflect the integration of emotional attunement with core principles of trauma-informed practice, which is significantly supported by research.

The four practices that follow provide focal points for you to consider as you strengthen these skills. While self-regulation is not specifically included as one of the practices, it is a crucial component of trauma-informed empathy:

Empathy is a relational skill, so your nervous system is a large part of the equation. Students will often mirror your energy, whether you are calm, afraid, or angry. Trauma-informed empathy can only be practiced when you are emotionally available.[6]

Ensuring that you have developed a level of mastery in self-regulation will result in the best outcome when using this tool.

Trauma-Informed Empathy Practices

 ## Reframe

When a person withdraws, lashes out, refuses to comply, or makes threats, pause and consider what they are trying to communicate. Also consider if the behavior may be a protective response. This practice engages your cognition, reduces blame, and activates curiosity.

 ## Recognize

Recognize survival responses (fight, flight, freeze) like clenched fists, darting eyes, collapsed posture, non-responsiveness, etc. and allow the person to move back into a more regulated state before engaging further. Additionally, recognize other signs of trauma like anxiety, moodiness, distrust, avoidance, and dysregulation.

 ## Contextualize

Individuals who have been traumatized often have compounding sources of trauma. Consider medical issues, sensory overwhelm, social rejection, academic failure and the like. Ask yourself, "What might this person be carrying emotionally that I cannot see?

 ## Focus

Focus on the need, not the behavior in isolation. Prioritize safety and connection over reacting assertively. Instead of thinking "How do I stop this disruptive behavior," ask "What does this person need to feel safe and seen?"

The second theme or practice of a trauma-informed empathy approach is to recognize indicators of the stress response and other indicators of trauma. An excellent resource from the National Child Traumatic Stress Network: *Child Trauma Toolkit for Educators* is a great way to gain insight into how trauma affects children. Take a moment to find this resource online and download the free copy for review. The website address is provided here:

https://www.nctsn.org/resources/child-trauma-toolkit-educators

Once downloaded, move to the primary grade level you work with: elementary, middle, or high school. If you are a district or state administrator, you may choose any grade level. Find the section that shares "What you might observe..." and answer the following questions in the space provided.

- Do you connect any of these descriptions in the *Child Trauma Toolkit for Educators* to a student or students you currently work with? If so, which descriptors stand out the most? If not, do the descriptors relate to any of your friends, colleagues, or family members? Which ones?
- Will you incorporate any of the trauma-informed empathy practices provided in this section? If so, which ones?

____

____

____

____

____

____

____

- Keep in mind that using Trauma-Informed Empathy (TIE) does not excuse bad behavior. Instead, it offers a different way to understand and approach behavior.
- When you recognize the stress response: fight, flight, or freeze, communicating demands will usually not result in compliant behavior. In fact, the opposite may occur in that the behavior may escalate. Wait until you notice some degree of de-escalation before attempting to gain compliance.
- Always debrief with the student after a behavioral incident. Discussing what happened when everyone is in a calm state helps you gain insight of the underlying causes of the behavior, what you might proactively do to prevent future episodes, and it builds trust between you and the traumatized individual.

Summary and Reflection

Empathy development is the first skill that connects internal mastery and human relationships. It integrates and moves awareness and regulation outward, leading to responses grounded in understanding, rather than assumptions.

Perspective taking shifts defensive reactions to thoughtful responses by intentionally viewing situations through another person's lens. Trauma-informed empathy cautions against assuming behavior stems from defiance or disrespect alone, and urges you to consider the effect of trauma on communication, stress responses, and the need for safety. This shift supports more effective and regulated responses during moments of conflict or crisis.

Active listening and Nonviolent Communication are additional empathy tools that further strengthen this skill set. Although these techniques were not explicitly covered in this workbook, they are explored in *Transformational Tools for Special Educators* (Corwin, 2026) and can also be examined through independent research.

As with all emotional intelligence skills, the consistent practice of empathy strengthens the neural networks that support attuned, intentional, and regulated responses over time.

Before moving to social skills activities, take a moment to briefly review this chapter and complete the reflection activity that follows.

- Do you feel that you are naturally empathetic? Describe what makes you feel that you are, or are not, empathetic by nature.

- When thinking about external skills, why is developing strong internal skills a necessary prerequisite?

- Are you willing to practice perspective-taking or Trauma-Informed Empathy in the coming weeks? If so, how will you integrate these practices? If not, why not?

Chapter 7
Social Skills Activities

Both empathy and social skills strengthen the bridge between your internal emotional world and external relationships. As an educator, your relationships with others directly affect the quality of your work life in numerous ways, including but not limited to:

- Student outcomes
- Your professional reputation
- Conflict and stress levels
- Support from colleagues, families, and leaders
- Success and advancement
- Staff retention
- Resilience in the field
- Quality of collaboration

While self-awareness illuminates what you're experiencing and self-regulation determines how you manage those experiences, social skills govern how you translate that internal mastery into collaborative action. Without these skills, even the most emotionally intelligent person struggles to build the trust, cooperation, and mutual understanding essential for educational environments.

Empathy and social skills development overlap, but they serve different functions. Empathy is your capacity to understand what someone else is experiencing and communicate that understanding. For example, when a parent expresses frustration about their child's progress, empathy allows you to recognize the fear or exhaustion behind that frustration and reflect it back: "I can see how concerning this is, especially given everything you're managing."

Social skills include empathetic communication but extend further into relationship management and strategic navigation. For example, what do you do after that empathetic acknowledgment? How do you structure the rest of the conversation? If you fundamentally disagree about the appropriate intervention, how do you move forward? These situations require social skills that build on empathy, but require additional competencies like conflict resolution, boundary-setting, and collaborative problem-solving.

It is not uncommon for a person to perfectly demonstrate empathy, yet still struggle with social skills. Understanding others deeply doesn't automatically translate into knowing how to navigate complex interpersonal dynamics, facilitate difficult conversations, or build sustainable working relationships under stress.

Where empathy and social skills share common ground is that both require one critical prerequisite: a level of competency in the internal skills provided in Part One. When you operate from a place of emotional overload or reactivity, you simply don't have the cognitive space to track what's actually happening in an interaction. This hinders your ability to read social cues accurately or respond strategically.

We will target the following research-based tools to develop social skills:

✓ **Conflict Resolution Strategies:** Provide structured methods for resolving disagreements in ways that preserve dignity and reinforce trust.

✓ **Social Awareness:** Recognizing and understanding the needs of others by increasing sensitivity to social cues and cultural differences.

Conflict Resolution Strategies

No matter the context of a relationship, conflict is inevitable. The question isn't whether conflict will occur; it is whether you have strategies to resolve it constructively. Poor conflict resolution can damage professional relationships and create toxic team dynamics. Skilled conflict resolution does the opposite: it strengthens trust and builds your reputation as someone colleagues trust and respect.

Most people default to one of three unproductive patterns when conflict emerges: avoidance (hoping the problem goes away or resolves itself), accommodation (giving in to preserve peace), or competition (trying to win). Each pattern creates different problems, and none builds sustainable solutions or relationships.

Effective conflict resolution requires specific strategies that help you address disagreement directly while maintaining relational integrity. The questions below will prompt you to think about your current patterns and feelings about conflict.

Circle the Best Answer.

1) In your work environment, how often do you experience conflict?
   Daily   Weekly   Monthly   Never

2) When you disagree with a colleague, which of the following is most true for you?
   Let it go | Push your point of view | Find common ground | Something else

3) When faced with conflict, which of the following is most true for you?
   I feel frustrated or angry | I feel offended | I get curious | I walk away | Something else

Most would agree that conflict never feels "good," but when you shift into a state of curiosity instead of feeling frustrated, you move away from an emotional reaction and into problem-solving mode. This truly makes all the difference and typically results in a neutral or positive outcome.

Take a moment to review the three techniques for effective conflict resolution and work through the practice activity that follows.

Conflict Resolution Strategies

Collaborative Problem-Solving

This method encourages all parties to share their perspectives, identify shared goals, and brainstorm solutions that benefit everyone involved. Rather than assigning blame, collaborative problem-solving focuses on creating win-win outcomes.

Using "we" statements instead of "you" statements is one way to approach this technique. For example, "How can we find a solution that works for both of us?"

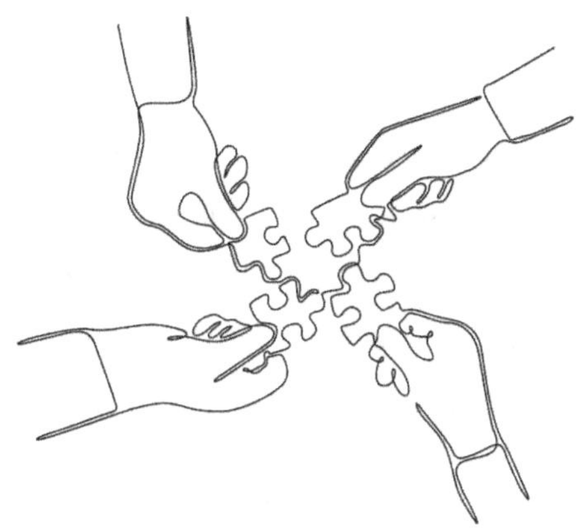

Assertive Communication

Assertive communication strikes a balance between passivity and aggression. This allows you to express thoughts and feelings clearly while also respecting others.

- Use statements, such as "I feel concerned when meetings start late because it disrupts my schedule,"
- Express your needs and boundaries confidently while remaining open to others' perspectives. For example, instead of saying, "That's fine, whatever you decide." You might say, "I'm feeling overwhelmed with last-minute changes. I really need more notice to support my students effectively."

Integrate Empathy

Integrating empathy tools when conflict arises ensures that all parties feel heard, understood, and respected. This plays a crucial role in resolving conflict.

- Give your full attention to the speaker, concentrating on what he or she is communicating, rather than focusing on how the information is delivered.
- Consider the situation from the speaker's point of view so that you can shift your own emotional response into a more deliberate approach.

Two scenarios are provided below. Each illustrates a charged interaction and a response that will likely amplify conflict. Read through each one, and using one of the conflict resolution techniques provided, craft a different response. Examples are provided at the end of each activity for your reference.

Scenario One:

A general education teacher approaches a special education teacher about a student on her caseload who is struggling to complete assignments and will likely fail. The special education teacher is immediately frustrated because during a recent IEP meeting, she recommended reducing assignments, but the general education teacher strongly opposed this, and the committee sided with her.

The special education teacher sharply states, *"This is exactly why I said we needed to lower his expectations in the IEP meeting, but you disagreed. If you had just followed my recommendations from the beginning, we wouldn't be dealing with this now. The modifications I suggested would have prevented all of this."*

- In situations like this, it can be helpful not to focus on who is right or who is wrong. After all, the ultimate goal is student success! Use ***collaborative problem-solving*** to revise the special educator's response. An example is provided below.

____

____

____

____

____

____

____

Scenario One: Example of a revised response using collaborative problem-solving
"This is frustrating for both of us. We both want this student to succeed. Can we sit down together and look at what's happening? Maybe we can identify which assignments are causing the most difficulty and brainstorm modifications that we're both comfortable with."

Scenario Two:

A principal schedules a mandatory curriculum planning meeting during a teacher's lunch period for the third time this month. The teacher has previously mentioned needing this time to prepare for afternoon classes.

The teacher rolls her eyes and says, _"Seriously? Oh, okay. Yeah, that's fine. Whatever works best for everyone else. I can just eat at my desk later and figure out the afternoon prep somehow. No big deal."_

- In this scenario, the ultimate goal is for the teacher to advocate for herself and her time. Using **assertive communication**, revise the teacher's response.

____

____

____

____

____

____

____

"I appreciate you letting me know. However, I'm concerned because this is the third time this month my lunch period has been used for meetings. I need that time to prepare for my afternoon classes and to recharge. Is there another time slot that could work for the team? I want to participate fully, but I also need to maintain what helps me be effective with my students."

After completing this activity, do you think your revised responses, or the example revisions provided, will change the outcome of the conflict? If so, how? If not, why not?

———————————————————————————

———————————————————————————

———————————————————————————

———————————————————————————

———————————————————————————

———————————————————————————

———————————————————————————

The most challenging part of using collaborative problem-solving in the moment is that intense situations can create automatic reactions. These reactions can occur before you have a moment to choose a better response, which is why keeping your self-regulation skills strong is essential. If you can self-regulate in difficult circumstances, then you have a moment to shift from reactivity to proactive problem-solving.

Social Awareness

Imagine a principal or school administrator calling a mandatory meeting fifteen minutes before teaching staff leave for the day. Teachers and support staff arrive to the meeting with their coats on, bags packed, visibly checking their phones and watches. Several staff members mention picking up kids from daycare.

The principal launches into a detailed 45-minute presentation, complete with a 20-slide PowerPoint, saying, "This is really important, so I want to make sure we cover everything thoroughly today." When teachers glance at each other and shift in their seats, the principal doesn't pause. When someone asks if there's a quick reference guide to review later, the principal responds, "Let's just go through it all now so everyone's on the same page," and continues for another 30 minutes.

If the principal's goal was to ensure that everyone both accessed and retained the important information presented, it is unlikely that the goal was met.

What the administrator missed:

- Nonverbal cues indicating time pressure
- Verbal hints about competing commitments
- Body language showing disengagement
- The request for alternative options signaled that the timing wasn't working for the group

Given the group's social signals, the information provided will not be fully retained. More than that, the group may feel that they have been disrespected because the meeting either added additional stress at the end of the day or cut into their personal time. These feelings will negatively affect their relationship with the administrator.

This scenario illustrates the importance of social awareness or "reading the room." Even if the administrator needed to share the information by a deadline, using social awareness in the same situation can make a huge difference.

A socially aware administrator might have prepared for a full presentation, but notices the coats, packed bags, and time-checking. Given the social cues, an aligned response might be:

I can see everyone's ready to head out. I know it's Friday afternoon and you all have places to be. I need about 10 minutes to give you the overview of our new documentation system. I will create a quick reference guide and share the presentation slides and video tutorial with you today, so that you can review them on your own time. Everyone must be clear on the essentials, but let me just hit the key points now, and then we can check in next week to make sure everyone is on the same page.

The principal covers only the essentials: what's changing, when it starts, and where to find resources. When finished in 12 minutes, the principal asks, "Any quick questions, or would you rather email me over the weekend?" Several teachers thank the principal for keeping it brief.

This approach makes staff members feel that their time is respected, and they are much more likely to learn and retain the information shared, because even though it was clear that the new process had to be learned, the option of learning on their own time has a better chance of meeting the administrator's ultimate goal, while also maintaining a positive relationship between staff members.

Educators juggle competing priorities, constant time pressure, and emotional labor throughout the day, which can make noticing and responding to social cues feel secondary or even impossible in the moment. Social awareness is not about being perfectly attuned at all times. It is about building the capacity to notice patterns and pause long enough to interpret what is happening around you. In doing so, you provide yourself the opportunity to adjust your response in ways that support both the task and the people involved.

Think about your level of social awareness and what factors may influence your competency by answering the questions below.

Social Awareness Check

Circle the Best Answer.

1) When faced with time constraints or mental overload, do you tend to turn inward and become less sensitive to social cues?

   Yes   No   Sometimes

2) Have you ever attended a group activity and noticed that the leader or speaker seemed out of touch with the audience?

   Yes   No

3) Self Assessment: How well do you read nonverbal and social cues?

   I struggle | I'm pretty good at it | I'm about average | I excel with this skill | Not sure

Even if you naturally excel with social awareness, you will find that the techniques that follow are designed to strengthen that capacity. Rather than asking for more effort or vigilance, they focus on developing practical awareness skills that can be applied in real situations without adding to an already full cognitive load.

Social Awareness Practices

Observational Exercises

Observational exercises place you in the role of "active observer." The goal is to focus on noticing body language, facial expressions, and group dynamics without immediate engagement.

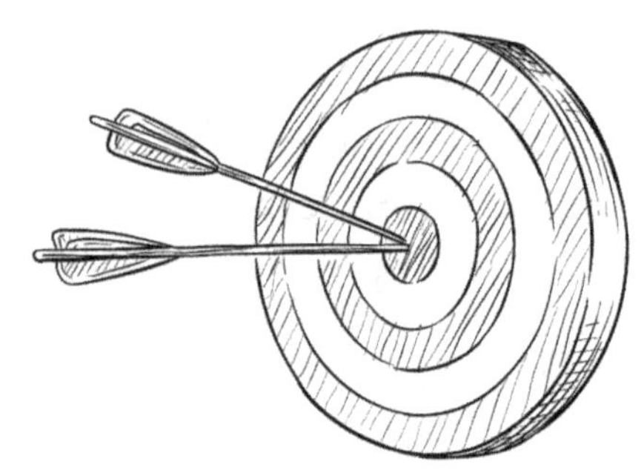

Attention Discipline:

-Set a clear intention before entering any social space. Decide what you want to notice, such as tone, posture, or group energy.

-As the interaction unfolds, keep your focus on what is happening in real time rather than what you think about it.

-Quiet your internal commentary by redirecting your attention each time your thoughts drift or you begin to judge what you're seeing.

-Stay mentally present by avoiding multitasking, and anchor your focus by watching carefully and listening fully.

-Use breathwork or grounding strategies to bring yourself back when your mind wanders. Afterward, take one minute to reflect on what you noticed.

This daily practice strengthens your ability to observe clearly and respond with insight.

Social Scanning & Delayed Analysis

-Choose any setting where social interaction is naturally occurring. This could be a classroom, staff meeting, or therapy session.

-Silently observe the dynamics without intervening. Focus your attention on physical and nonverbal cues such as posture, eye contact, facial expressions, body orientation, and tone. Pay attention to how individuals initiate or respond to others—notice who dominates the conversation, who withdraws, and who appears engaged or disconnected. Observe everyone and not just fixating one person.

-Take notes for later analysis.

-Resist the urge to label behaviors or assume motives. Instead, record exactly what you see and hear. For example, instead of writing "He was frustrated," note "He crossed his arms, exhaled audibly, and looked away when asked to respond."

After observing multiple times, analyze and look for patterns.

Practicing Attention Discipline and Social Scanning requires a group setting, so it cannot be directly applied here. However, the reflection questions below can help uncover any barriers that might hinder your social awareness competency.

- In your work environment, do you find it difficult to give your full attention to a group activity or meeting? If so, what is your primary distractor? If not, how do you manage to stay fully engaged?
- After a meeting or group interaction, do you reflect on the tone and mood of the meeting, or do you tend to move on without thinking about it?
- Self-regulation is an imperative component of "reading the room" correctly. Why do you think this skill is crucial for social awareness?

____

____

____

____

____

____

____

Cultural Competence

Along with strengthening your ability to notice nonverbal and social cues, social awareness also involves developing cultural competence. Culture influences how people communicate, interpret behavior, and respond to authority, time, and relationships.

Expanding cultural awareness allows you to read situations more accurately and respond with greater empathy and flexibility. Participating in meaningful conversations and learning from diverse perspectives deepens awareness of social nuance beyond your own experiences.

An easy way to build this mindset is to examine how your own background has shaped your values, assumptions, and communication style. The short activity below offers a basic format for this type of reflection, but it is just a starting point, and you are encouraged to dig deeper into your own cultural influences!

PRACTICE

Reflect on what was emphasized in your childhood home and answer the following questions in the space provided.

- How was respect defined in your childhood home?
- What did you learn about authority as a child? Were you taught to respect authority, challenge it, or something else?
- What were the expectations of men, women, and children in your home?
- How did your home values differ from those of your peers? How were they the same?

____

____

____

____

____

____

____

Understanding how your culture shapes your perspectives is the foundation. From there, seek conversations with people from different cultural backgrounds and approach with genuine curiosity to listen and learn. These exchanges will expand your awareness of others while revealing insights about yourself and your own culture. After each conversation, reflect on what challenged your assumptions and what you'll carry forward.

This practice builds the social awareness needed for responsive engagement in diverse settings.

Summary and Reflection

Social skills extend empathy into action by supporting collaborative problem solving, conflict reduction, and establishing healthy boundaries. Effective conflict resolution allows you to address disagreement directly while maintaining personal integrity and respect for others. When all parties are encouraged to share perspectives and clarify goals, relationships strengthen through solutions that support mutual benefit. Social awareness sharpens your ability to read the room with accuracy, allowing you to respond in ways that are attuned, intentional, and aligned with both the emotional climate and the needs of the moment.

When empathy and social skills are fully integrated, the tone of a workplace shifts in noticeable ways. Conversations become more honest without assigning blame. Tension is addressed before it becomes resentment. People listen with the intent to understand rather than to defend, and this creates a supportive culture where all staff members can thrive.

Consider the content provided in this chapter and complete the short reflection that follows.

- Do you use conflict resolution strategies in your work environment? If so, which ones? If not, are you willing to practice the strategies offered here?

- What are your thoughts on developing social awareness skills? Explain why these skills are important when it comes to relationship building.

- How might cultivating social skills improve your professional and personal relationships?

Moving Forward

Developing emotional intelligence as a core professional skill set requires a commitment to consistency. It is helpful to begin with one or two tools or techniques that you resonated with most and apply your practice during a specific time each day. Many of the tools covered in this workbook take less than ten minutes to complete, and structuring them as a daily practice makes follow-through reliable. With consistent engagement, broader integration becomes possible.

Once your selected practices become habitual, adding additional tools is more manageable, and over time, tools across the five domains begin to work together in ways that deepen their individual effect. Simply put, each domain naturally reinforces the others. You will notice the interconnected relationship of the five domains in the moment before a reaction, in the recovery time after a difficult encounter, and in the quality of the relationships you build and sustain over time.

Be sure to mark your calendar and return to your EERC and MBI scores at the three and six-month intervals noted at the beginning of this workbook and use those scores alongside your chapter reflections to assess where growth has occurred and where continued focus is warranted.

The research base behind each tool presented here extends well beyond what a single workbook can convey, and exploring that evidence will deepen both your understanding and your application of these practices over time.

About the Author

Katrina G. Huels is an educational consultant and former special education leader with more than twenty years of experience working across classrooms, programs, and district leadership. Her work focuses on helping educators sustain their passion and effectiveness in one of the most emotionally demanding fields.

Drawing on a background in psychology, neuroscience-informed practice, and educational leadership, Katrina translates research into practical tools educators can use in the middle of a demanding school day. Her work centers on emotional intelligence development, neuroplasticity, and the cultivation of professional resilience.

Katrina is the author of *Transformational Tools for Special Educators* (Corwin, 2026) and *The Motivation Toolkit* (Applied Harmony, 2025). She is the creator of *Applied Harmony*, an initiative focused on helping educators build inner mastery and long-term professional sustainability through emotional intelligence development. Her work advocates for emotional intelligence training to be recognized not as a wellness trend, but as a professional competency that strengthens school culture, educator retention, and student outcomes.

Learn more at www.huelsappliedharmony.com

Notes

Beginning the Work

1. Maurice J. Elias, Mary Utne O'Brien, and Roger P. Weissberg, "Transformative Leadership for Social-Emotional Learning," *Principal Leadership* 7, no. 4 (2006): 10–13; Kimberly A. Schonert-Reichl, "Social and Emotional Learning and Teachers," *The Future of Children* 27, no. 1 (Spring 2017): 137–155.

2. Sergio Mérida López and Natalio Extremera, "Emotional Intelligence and Teacher Burnout: A Systematic Review," *International Journal of Educational Research* 85 (2017): 121–130; Yi Wang, Fengyu Zai, and Xiaoyong Zhou, "The Impact of Emotion Regulation Strategies on Teachers' Well Being and Positive Emotions: A Meta Analysis," *Behavioral Sciences* 15, no. 3 (2025): 342.

3. Karni, Asher, Dov Sagi, Moshe Jezzard, Michael M. Anderson, Alan J. Brooks, and David G. Gadian. "Functional MRI Evidence for Adult Motor Cortex Plasticity During Motor Skill Learning." *Proceedings of the National Academy of Sciences of the United States of America* 95, no. 3 (1998): 861–868.

4. Patricia A. Jennings and Mark T. Greenberg, "The Prosocial Classroom: Teacher Social and Emotional Competence in Relation to Student and Classroom Outcomes," *Review of Educational Research* 79, no. 1 (2009): 491-525.

2. Self-Awareness Activities

1. Robert A. Emmons and Michael E. McCullough, "Counting Blessings versus Burdens: An Experimental Investigation of Gratitude and Subjective Well-Being in Daily Life," *Journal of Personality and Social Psychology* 84, no. 2 (2003): 377 to 389; Karen O'Leary and Samantha Dockray, "The Effects of Two Novel Gratitude and Mindfulness Interventions on Well-Being," *Journal of Alternative and Complementary Medicine* 21, no. 4 (2015): 243 to 245; Marta Jackowska, Jennie Brown, Amy Ronaldson, and Andrew Steptoe, "The Impact of a Brief Gratitude Intervention on Subjective Well-Being, Biology and Sleep," *Journal of Health Psychology* 21, no. 10 (2016): 2207 to 2217; Glenn R. Fox, Jo-Ann K. Kaplan, and Antonio Damasio, "Neural Correlates of Gratitude," *Frontiers in Psychology* 6 (2015): 1491; Sara B. Algoe, "Find, Remind, and Bind: The Functions of Gratitude in Everyday Relationships," *Social and Personality Psychology Compass* 6, no. 6 (2012): 455 to 469.

2. Marta Jackowska, Jennie Brown, Amy Ronaldson, and Andrew Steptoe, "The Impact of a Brief Gratitude Intervention on Subjective Well-Being, Biology and Sleep," *Journal of Health Psychology* 21, no. 10 (2016): 2207 to 2217; Karen O'Leary and Samantha Dockray, "The Effects of Two Novel Gratitude and Mindfulness Interventions on Well-Being," *Journal of Alternative and Complementary Medicine* 21, no. 4 (2015): 243 to 245.

3. James W. Pennebaker and Joshua M. Smyth, *Opening Up by Writing It Down: How Expressive Writing Improves Health and Eases Emotional Pain*, 3rd ed. (New York: Guilford Press, 2016); Karen A. Baikie and Kay Wilhelm, "Emotional and Physical Health Benefits of Expressive Writing," *Advances in Psychiatric Treatment* 11, no. 5 (2005): 338–346.

4. Katrina G. Huels, *Transformational Tools for Special Educators: How to Beat Burnout and Become the Best at What You Do* (Corwin, 2026).

3. Self-Regulation Activities

1. Melis Y. Balban et al., "Brief Structured Respiration Practices Enhance Mood and Reduce Physiological Arousal," *Cell Reports Medicine* 4, no. 1 (January 2023): 100895.

4. Motivation Activities

1. Katrina G. Huels, *The Motivation Toolkit: Cultivate Your Inner Drive* (Independently published, 2025).
2. Katrina G. Huels, *Transformational Tools for Special Educators* (Corwin, 2026), 103.
3. Ibid.
4. Katrina G. Huels, *Transformational Tools for Special Educators: How to Beat Burnout and Become the Best at What You Do* (Thousand Oaks, CA: Corwin, 2026).

6. Empathy Activities

1. Katrina G. Huels, *Transformational Tools for Special Educators: How to Beat Burnout and Become the Best at What You Do* (Thousand Oaks, CA: Corwin, 2026).
2. Jane W. Pelcovitz et al., "Child Maltreatment in Children with Medical Complexity and Disability," *Current Problems in Pediatric and Adolescent Health Care* 54, no. 5 (May 2024): 101548.
3. Evelyne C. P. Offerman et al., "Prevalence of Adverse Childhood Experiences in Students with Emotional and Behavioral Disorders in Special Education Schools from a Multi-Informant Perspective," *International Journal of Environmental Research and Public Health* 19, no. 6 (March 2022): 3411.
4. The Problem: Impact," Trauma Sensitive Schools, accessed January 26, 2026.
5. Jessica B. Koslouski, "Developing Empathy and Support for Students with the 'Most Challenging Behaviors': Mixed-Methods Outcomes of Professional Development in Trauma-Informed Teaching Practices," *Frontiers in Education* 7 (2022): Article 1005887.
6. Katrina G. Huels, *Transformational Tools for Special Educators: How to Beat Burnout and Become the Best at What You Do* (Thousand Oaks, CA: Corwin, 2026).

9 798999 617670 0